Trading Baseball Cards

Learning the Symbols +, −, and =

Jessica Baron

Math for the REAL World™

Rosen Classroom Books & Materials
New York

Charles, Karen, and Brian like to trade baseball cards. They use math when they trade baseball cards. They add and subtract.

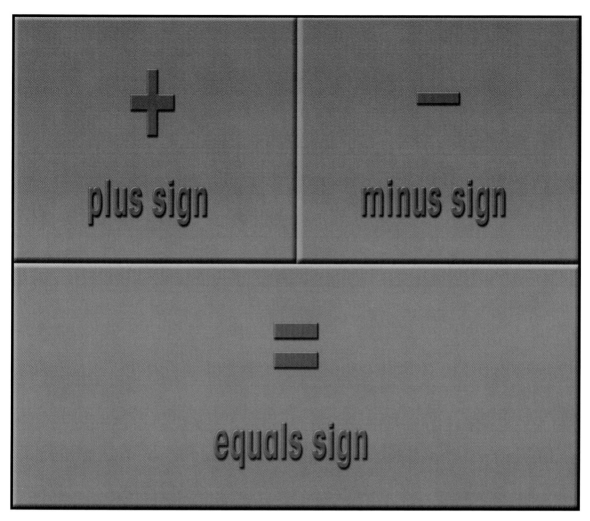

plus sign

minus sign

equals sign

A plus sign is used for adding. A minus sign is used for subtracting. An equals sign helps to show how many there are after adding or subtracting.

Charles has 10 cards. Brian gives him 2 more cards. Now Charles has 12 cards.

10 cards + 2 cards = 12 cards

Charles gives Brian 2 cards in return.

Now Charles has 10 cards again.

12 cards – 2 cards = 10 cards

Brian has 7 cards. Karen gives him 3 more cards. Now Brian has 10 cards.

7 cards + 3 cards = 10 cards

Brian gives Karen 3 cards in return.

Now Brian has 7 cards again.

10 cards − 3 cards = 7 cards

Karen has 5 cards. Charles gives her 5 more cards. Now Karen has 10 cards.

5 cards + 5 cards = 10 cards

Karen gives Charles 5 cards in return.

Now Karen has 5 cards again.

10 cards – 5 cards = 5 cards

Charles has 10 cards. He gives 5 cards
to Brian. Now Charles has 5 cards.

10 cards – 5 cards = 5 cards

Brian gives Charles 5 cards in return.

Now Charles has 10 cards again.

5 cards + 5 cards = 10 cards

Words to Know

baseball cards

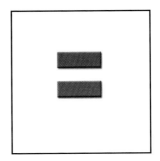
equals sign

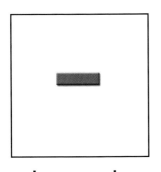
minus sign

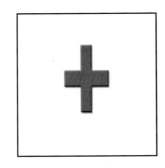
plus sign

trade